NATIONAL GEOGRAPHIC | **GLOBAL ISSUES**

ENERGY
RESOURCES

Andrew J. Milson, Ph.D.
Content Consultant
University of Texas at Arlington

Acknowledgments

Grateful acknowledgment is given to the authors, artists, photographers, museums, publishers, and agents for permission to reprint copyrighted material. Every effort has been made to secure the appropriate permission. If any omissions have been made or if corrections are required, please contact the Publisher.

Instructional Consultant: Christopher Johnson, Evanston, Illinois

Teacher Reviewer: Andrea Wallenbeck, Exploris Middle School, Raleigh, North Carolina

Photographic Credits

Front Cover, Inside Front Cover, Title Page (bg) ©Chris McKay/National Geographic Stock. **3** (bg) ©Manoj Shah/Stone/Getty Images. **4** (bg) ©Deepol/Rudi Sebastian/plainpicture. **6** (bg) ©Roger Eritja/Alamy. **8** (bg) Mapping Specialists. **10** (bg) ©Jane Sweeney/Robert Harding World Imagery/Corbis. **11** (tl) Mapping Specialists. **12** (cr) ©Luis Castañeda/age fotostock. **13** (bg) Precision Graphics. **15** (bg) ©REUTERS/Leonardo Morais-Light Press (BRAZIL). **16** (bg) ©RIA Novosti/Photo Researchers, Inc. **19** (bg) ©Galen Rowell/Corbis. **20** (bg) ©ITAR-TASS/Igor Buimistrov/Newscom. (tl) ©Natalia Kolesnikova/AFP/Getty Images. **22** (bg) ©Andrew Castellano. **23** (bl) ©Thomas Culhane/SolarCities. **24** (cr) ©Andrew Castellano. **25** (bg) ©Andrew Castellano. **27** (t) ©Bob Daemmrich/Corbis. **28** (tr) ©David R. Frazier Photolibrary, Inc./Alamy. **30** (br) ©RIA Novosti/Photo Researchers, Inc. **31** (bg) ©Manoj Shah/Stone/Getty Images. (bl) ©Jane Sweeney/Robert Harding World Imagery/Corbis. (br) ©Lester Lefkowitz/Getty Images. (tl) ©Roger Eritja/Alamy. (tr) ©Luis Castañeda/age fotostock.

MetaMetrics® and the MetaMetrics logo and tagline are trademarks of MetaMetrics, Inc., and are registered in the United States and abroad. The trademarks and names of other companies and products mentioned herein are the property of their respective owners. Copyright © 2010 MetaMetrics, Inc. All rights reserved.

Visit National Geographic Learning online at www.NGSP.com.

Visit our corporate website at www.cengage.com.

ISBN: 978-07362-97622

Printed in the United States of America
Print Number: 07   Print Year: 2023

ENERGY TO POWER THE WO

Energy production in Hamburg, Germany, has filled the skies with air pollution.

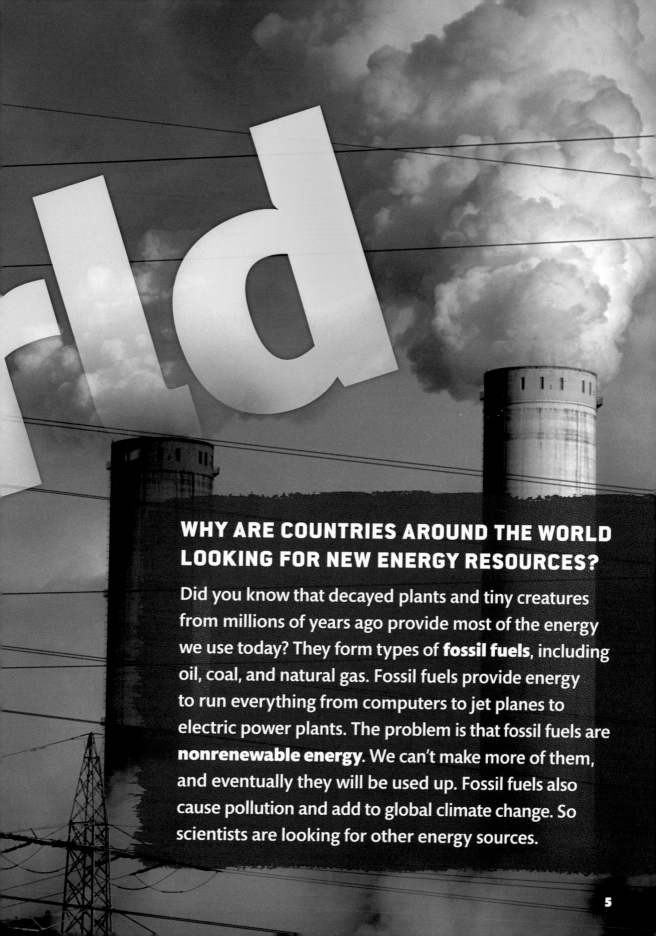

WHY ARE COUNTRIES AROUND THE WORLD LOOKING FOR NEW ENERGY RESOURCES?

Did you know that decayed plants and tiny creatures from millions of years ago provide most of the energy we use today? They form types of **fossil fuels**, including oil, coal, and natural gas. Fossil fuels provide energy to run everything from computers to jet planes to electric power plants. The problem is that fossil fuels are **nonrenewable energy**. We can't make more of them, and eventually they will be used up. Fossil fuels also cause pollution and add to global climate change. So scientists are looking for other energy sources.

FOSSIL FUEL FACTS

Every single day the world burns about 3.6 billion gallons of oil. That's enough to fill almost 122 million bathtubs! New sources of fossil fuels are getting harder to find and get out of the earth.

Producing and burning fossil fuels hurts the environment. Gases released by burning fossil fuels in power plants or cars can lead to health problems. They can also cause water pollution. Some gases may also contribute to global climate change.

The Hoover Dam on the Colorado River has one of the largest hydroelectric power plants in the world.

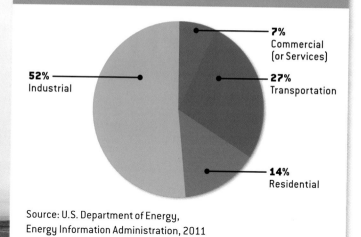

WORLD ENERGY USE BY SECTOR

- 7% Commercial (or Services)
- 27% Transportation
- 52% Industrial
- 14% Residential

Source: U.S. Department of Energy, Energy Information Administration, 2011

IS THERE ANOTHER CHOICE?

Scientists are looking at **renewable energy** to replace fossil fuels. These are resources that can be used without being used up. Water, sun, wind, and plants are renewable energy sources.

Renewable energy has many advantages. For example, it is almost unlimited. It's cleaner and generally does not pollute the air or water. And renewable energy sources don't release carbon dioxide (CO_2) into the air. Carbon dioxide is one of the gases that causes air pollution. It may be a factor in global climate change.

RENEWABLE ENERGY

If renewable energy has all these benefits, then why don't people use more of it? It's hard and costly to capture energy from water, the sun, or wind and get it to where it is needed. Most renewable energy is used to make electricity. Most vehicles and power plants, however, use fuel made from oil.

On the following pages, you will read about energy in Brazil and Russia. Brazil is looking into ways to use waterpower as an energy source. Using that power could help many people who live far from the usual energy sources. Russia has supplies of fossil fuels but the leaders know that the supply won't last forever. So it makes sense to start developing alternative energy sources. Russia's goal is to increase renewable energy use to 21 percent of all energy by 2020. Both Russia and Brazil want to use more renewable energy to power their growth.

Explore the Issue

1. **Make Inferences** What are three problems with using fossil fuels?

2. **Draw Conclusions** Why has renewable energy been more expensive than fossil fuels?

Energy Challeng

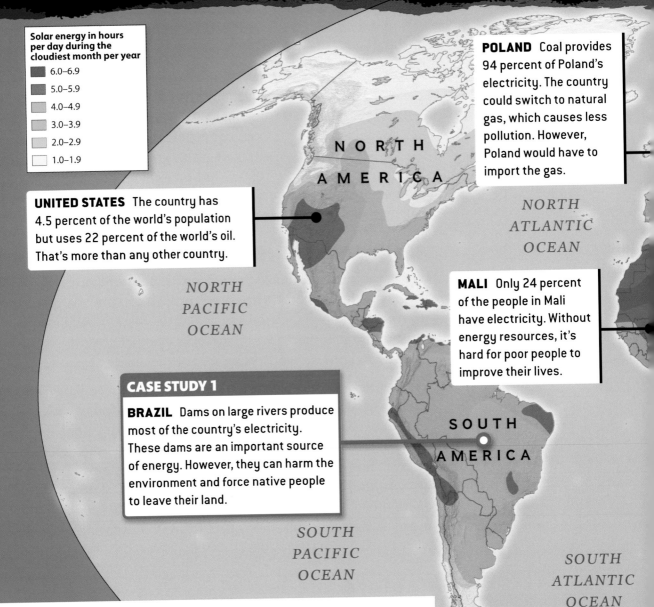

Solar energy in hours per day during the cloudiest month per year

- 6.0–6.9
- 5.0–5.9
- 4.0–4.9
- 3.0–3.9
- 2.0–2.9
- 1.0–1.9

POLAND Coal provides 94 percent of Poland's electricity. The country could switch to natural gas, which causes less pollution. However, Poland would have to import the gas.

UNITED STATES The country has 4.5 percent of the world's population but uses 22 percent of the world's oil. That's more than any other country.

MALI Only 24 percent of the people in Mali have electricity. Without energy resources, it's hard for poor people to improve their lives.

CASE STUDY 1

BRAZIL Dams on large rivers produce most of the country's electricity. These dams are an important source of energy. However, they can harm the environment and force native people to leave their land.

NORTH AMERICA

NORTH ATLANTIC OCEAN

NORTH PACIFIC OCEAN

SOUTH AMERICA

SOUTH PACIFIC OCEAN

SOUTH ATLANTIC OCEAN

Explore the Issue

1. **Interpret Maps** Which two continents have the best potential for using solar energy?

2. **Make Predictions** How do you think the decline of oil production in Siberia might affect Russia?

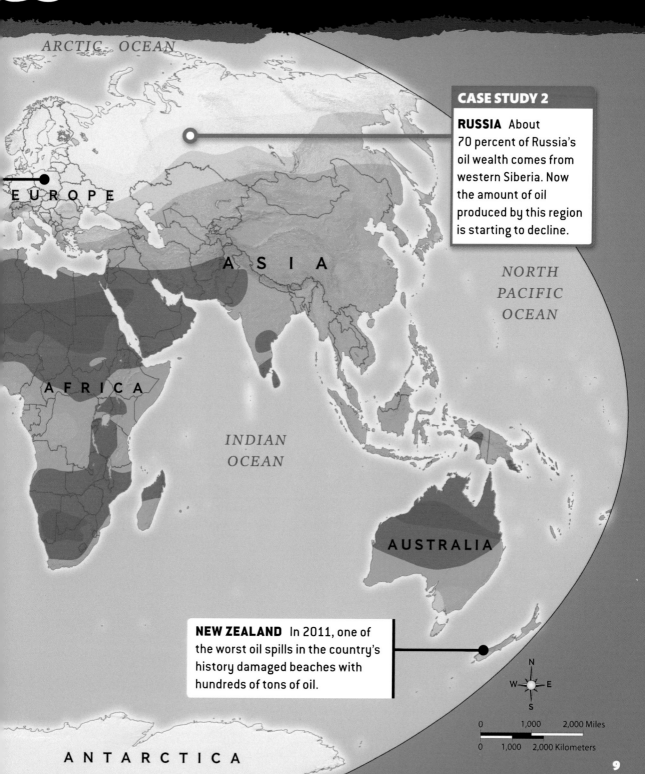

ARCTIC OCEAN

EUROPE

ASIA

AFRICA

NORTH
PACIFIC
OCEAN

INDIAN
OCEAN

AUSTRALIA

ANTARCTICA

CASE STUDY 2

RUSSIA About
70 percent of Russia's
oil wealth comes from
western Siberia. Now
the amount of oil
produced by this region
is starting to decline.

NEW ZEALAND In 2011, one of
the worst oil spills in the country's
history damaged beaches with
hundreds of tons of oil.

| 0 | | 1,000 | 2,000 Miles |
| 0 | | 1,000 | 2,000 Kilometers |

N
W E
S

9

Harnessing
WATER
in Bra

Iguacu Falls on the border of Argentina and Brazil is one of many waterfalls in Brazil. Using the power of falling water is a renewable energy option.

The map shows how rich Brazil is in waterpower resources.

THE POWER OF MOVING WATER

Moving water is powerful. Anyone who's ridden a raft down a rushing river or stood near a roaring waterfall can feel that power. People have used the power of moving water for thousands of years. Waterfalls turned wheels that ground wheat into flour. Early factories used waterpower to run their machines.

Hydroelectric power, or hydropower, is electricity produced by moving water. The water pressure spins the blades of engines called **turbines**. The turbines power **generators**, which are machines that produce electricity. The first hydroelectric power plants started in the late 1800s. Today, hydroelectric power is the world's largest renewable source of electricity.

Brazil is rich in waterpower resources. The mighty Amazon River flows mainly through Brazil. Other powerful Brazilian rivers include the Parana (par-rah-NAH) and São Francisco (SOW frann-SEE-zoh). These rivers provide about one-third of Brazil's total energy needs and almost all of its electricity.

BRAZIL'S ENERGY NEEDS

Brazil is a big country with growing energy needs. It's the fifth largest country in the world, both in area and in people. This huge country consumes more energy than any other country in South America. In fact, it's the ninth largest consumer of energy in the world.

Since 2000, Brazil's economy has been growing rapidly. It's the largest in South America. A growing economy means a growing need for energy. The country needs about one-third more energy than it did in the past.

Slightly more than half of Brazil's energy comes from fossil fuels, mostly oil. The country has been expanding its oil production. It now produces more than it needs, so it can export oil to other countries. For the time being, Brazil can rely on fossil fuels. Eventually, however, the supply of these fuels will run out.

HYDROPOWER IN BRAZIL

Most of Brazil's hydroelectricity comes from large power plants located on major rivers. The Itaipu (LTAY-poo) Dam, on the border between Brazil and Paraguay, is the second largest dam in the world. This hydropower plant provides about one-quarter of Brazil's hydroelectric power and about three-quarters of Paraguay's.

In order to build the dam, engineers had to move the course of the Parana River. The dam complex across the river is almost five miles wide. The **reservoir**, or artificial lake created behind the dam, stores water until it is needed.

These large dams create artificial waterfalls to produce electricity. The water flowing over the dam's turbines makes electricity, just as a natural waterfall does. People control how much water flows over the dam and the amount of electricity produced.

Water pours over the spillways of a hydroelectric dam in Brazil.

PROS AND CONS OF HYDROPOWER

Hydropower is a renewable energy source. Rain and melting snow usually refill the rivers each year. Hydroelectric generators do not pollute the air the way fossil fuel power plants do. Hydropower is the cheapest way to produce electricity, even though building large dams is expensive.

Although they produce clean, renewable energy, large dams can cause problems. Building a dam across a river may harm wildlife and plants in and along the river. Fish that swim upstream to lay their eggs can be blocked by dams. Building special ladders can help fish swim upstream.

Creating reservoirs can cause problems, too. Reservoirs may flood land that was used for farming. Reservoirs can also destroy land that is important for its historical sites or natural features. Sometimes, large numbers of people who live on the land have to relocate. Brazil has to weigh these factors when it decides to build a dam.

❺ TRANSMISSION LINES
Carry power to homes and businesses

DOWNSTREAM OUTLET

HOW HYDROPOWER WORKS

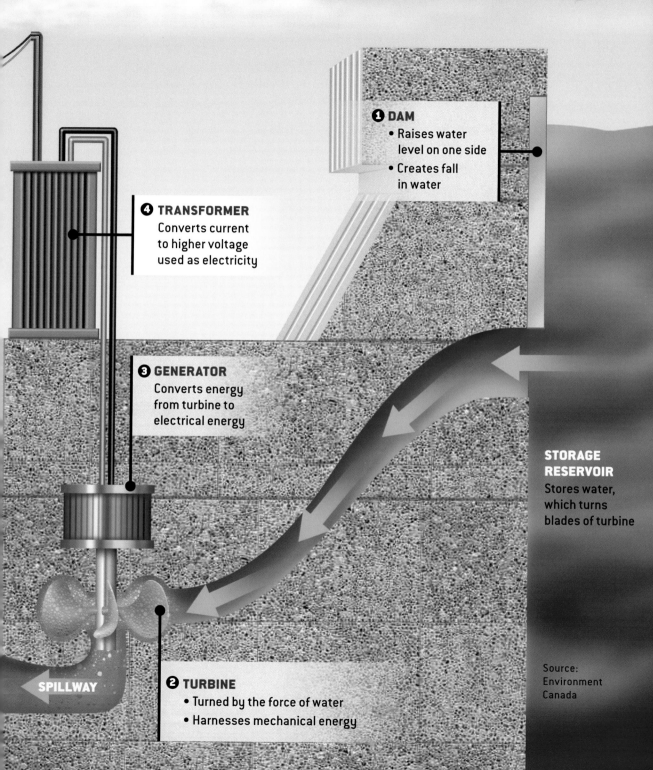

❶ DAM
- Raises water level on one side
- Creates fall in water

❹ TRANSFORMER
Converts current to higher voltage used as electricity

❸ GENERATOR
Converts energy from turbine to electrical energy

STORAGE RESERVOIR
Stores water, which turns blades of turbine

SPILLWAY

❷ TURBINE
- Turned by the force of water
- Harnesses mechanical energy

Source: Environment Canada

HYDROPOWER IN THE RAIN FOREST

In the mid-1980s, Brazil built the first large hydroelectric plant in the Amazon rain forest. The huge Tucurui (Too-KYURR-oo-ee) Dam on the Tocantins River produces hydroelectricity for most of two states, including nearby mines. However, building the dam flooded about 927 square miles of rain forest. About 30,000 native people had to leave their traditional land.

Environmental groups and native people oppose plans to build other large dams in the Amazon basin. In February 2010, the government approved the building of the Belo Monte dam on the Xingu (shin-GOO) River. The government agrees that about 193 square miles of rain forest will be flooded. Officials claim that native people will not have to leave their land. They say that native people's lives will be healthier after the dam is built. A leader of the Kayapo (Kay-AP-poo) Indians says, "We are opposed to dams on the Xingu and will fight to protect our river."

SMALL IS BEAUTIFUL

Millions of people who live in remote parts of the Amazon rain forest want access to electricity. It's expensive to try to extend the country's electrical system to these areas. Problems with large dams are causing some people to look for other solutions.

One solution is to construct smaller dams. A U.S. government agency helped build a small hydroelectric system in one of these remote villages. The system uses a natural waterfall that drops about 15 feet to power a small turbine. Other communities can now use this system as a model. In fact, Brazil plans to build many smaller hydropower plants throughout the country in the coming years. Millions could then benefit from renewable hydropower without damage to the environment.

Explore the Issue

1. **Make Generalizations** What are the benefits of hydropower for Brazil?

2. **Analyze Problems and Solutions** How does Brazil plan to bring electricity to people in the Amazon rain forest?

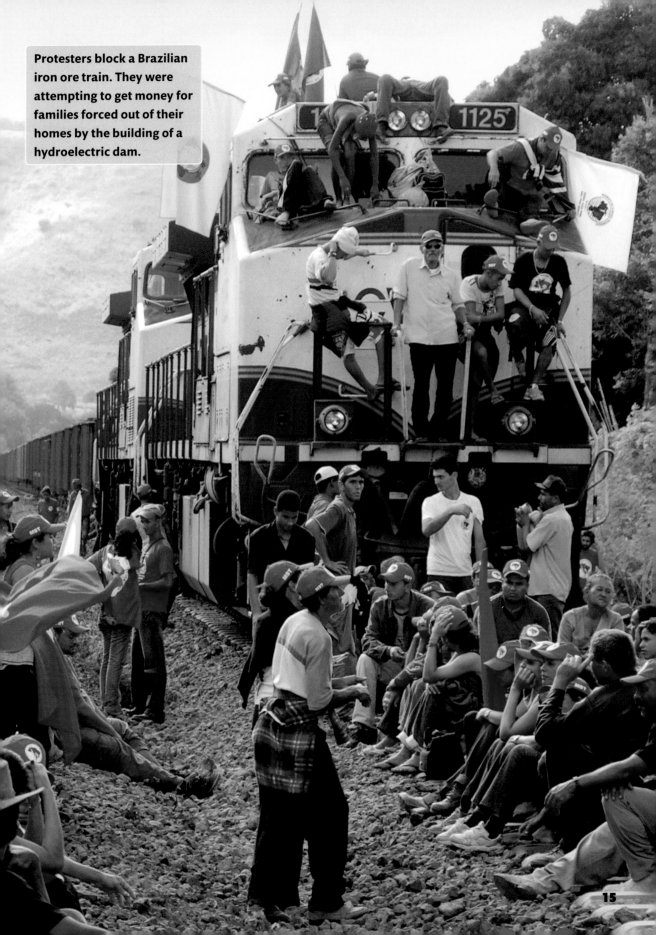

Protesters block a Brazilian iron ore train. They were attempting to get money for families forced out of their homes by the building of a hydroelectric dam.

Russian oil rig workers place machinery that will drill deep into the earth to tap oil reserves.

Russia's Vast ENERGY WEALTH

CELEBRATING OIL

Every September, people in western Siberia celebrate Oiler's Day. They gather in cities throughout Khanty-Mansi (KAHN-tee MANN-see) province to sing songs, dance, and release balloons. This holiday honors oil workers who have made the region—and the Russian government—wealthy.

Siberia is one of the harshest places on Earth. Temperatures can reach 60 degrees below zero Fahrenheit, with only a few hours of daylight in the middle of winter. In summer, mosquitoes pester people. Yet the oil industry there attracts many workers who want a better life.

People in the region have good reason to celebrate oil. Oil prices are ten times higher than in 1998. Oil wealth has transformed many towns. In the capital of Khanty-Mansi, a new airport terminal replaced a wooden shack. People enjoy new museums, restaurants, and sports facilities. All of these improvements have come from oil profits.

A FOSSIL FUEL GIANT

Russia is rich in fossil fuel resources. It competes with Saudi Arabia as the largest producer and exporter of oil in the world. About 70 percent of Russia's oil currently comes from western Siberia. The region's climate makes getting the oil resources a challenge.

Russia also contains the largest known reserves of natural gas in the world. **Natural gas** is a colorless, odorless, and tasteless gas. It is used for things such as heating, cooking, and making electricity. Like other fossil fuels, it is trapped in rocks underground or under the ocean. **Reserves** are the amount of a resource that can be recovered from known sources. With its huge reserves, Russia will be one of the world's largest exporters of natural gas for many years to come.

In Russia, the government controls the production and distribution of its energy resources. Exporting oil and natural gas is the main reason the country's economy has grown since 1998. Russia's neighbors in Central Asia and in Europe depend on Russian oil and natural gas for energy supplies. As their economies grow, so will the demand for more energy resources. Russia is determined to meet those demands.

BENEFITS OF AN ENERGY ECONOMY

About one-third of the Russian government **revenue**, or income, comes from the sale of oil and natural gas. These products are heavily taxed. For example, if the price of a barrel of oil is $100, the government takes $75 of the sale price in taxes. This money allows the country to invest in roads, schools, and national defense. Some money goes to the governments of provinces such as Khanty-Mansi. The money is used to build modern homes, shopping centers, and hospitals.

CHALLENGES OF AN ENERGY ECONOMY

Russia faces challenges, however, by having so much of its economy based on fossil fuels. For one thing, these nonrenewable resources will eventually be used up. These fields have been producing oil since the 1960s. Now the amount of oil they produce each year is starting to run out. It has also become more expensive to get oil from these fields.

Russia is a huge country, and most of its people live west of the Ural Mountains. However, most of its oil and gas reserves are located east of the mountains. So the energy is far from the Russians who need it. It is also far from customers in Europe. The distance makes it difficult and expensive to transport the oil and gas to the customers.

Russia also faces another risk in having so much of its economy tied up in energy. The country benefits from rising energy prices. When those prices go down, Russia's economy struggles. During the economic hard times in 2008 and 2009, oil prices dropped and the economy suffered. Russia needs to diversify, or broaden its economy, to get revenue from other sources. For example, the country is rich in other natural resources that are in demand around the world. Selling those resources will broaden the economy and be a new source of revenue. Some experts advise a move into areas such as science and computer technology.

Russia's energy is far from the Russians who need it.

Chukchi Peninsula in Russia is the location of untapped oil reserves, as well as home to herds of reindeer. Some people fear oil drilling will harm the environment here.

Demonstrators dressed as wind turbines call for the development of renewable energy sources.

A geothermal power station captures the heat from inside the earth to generate energy. Pictured here is a geothermal plant in Mutnovo, Russia, located in the far eastern part of Russia.

NEW FOSSIL FUEL SOURCES

Even though Russia is looking to diversify its economy, it is also exploring new sources of fossil fuels. Large reserves of oil are located in the eastern parts of the country. However, it will be more expensive to get this oil out of the ground than it has been in western Siberia. New pipelines will be needed to get this oil to customers. These exports will help Russia increase trade with its neighbors in East Asia.

The Caspian Sea is another area that is rich in oil and natural gas. Russia is making deals with its neighbors for new pipelines so it can control the transport of the Caspian's natural gas. For example, Russia will import natural gas from Kazakhstan (kah-ZAKH-stan) and Turkmenistan. Then it will export the gas to Europe at a profit.

RUSSIA'S RENEWABLE FUTURE

Russia wants to greatly increase its use of renewable energy by 2020. One big benefit of renewable energy is that it can be produced closer to the people who are using it. This makes renewable energy less costly. Different types of renewable energy are found in different parts of the country.

For example, the best areas for using wind energy are along the eastern coast and in the **steppes**, large grassy plains along the Volga River. Wind farms contain tall wind turbines used to produce electricity.

Russia can also use geothermal energy on some Pacific Islands and in areas near the Caucasus Mountains. **Geothermal energy** is the heat from inside the earth. In the form of steam or hot water, this energy heats buildings or generates electricity. Hydroelectric power is also a source of energy. Because the country is so large there are many opportunities to use this type of energy. Russia hopes to increase its energy wealth with all these renewable resources.

Explore the Issue

1. **Draw Conclusions** Why does Russia need to become less dependent on oil and natural gas?

2. **Analyze Solutions** How will renewable energy help Russia in the future?

Clean Energy
Improves Lives

T. H. Culhane talks to a resident of Nairobi, Kenya, about burning biogas instead of corn cobs.

CITY LIVING OFF THE GRID

In some poor neighborhoods of Cairo, Egypt's capital, a mother spends all day getting water to bathe her family. First, she walks to the water pipe in the center of her neighborhood. After filling her bucket, she walks back with it balanced on her head and climbs three flights of stairs to her apartment. There she dumps the bucket into a pot heating on her stove. She repeats this process many times, until there's enough warm water. When their days are spent in this way, women have no time to go to school or work to improve their lives.

Most people in cities in developed countries live "on the grid." This means their homes are connected to electricity and clean running water. When we think of living "off the grid," we usually think of people in rural areas. Could ideas from these rural people help people living without electricity in cities?

FROM TREETOPS TO ROOFTOPS

That was just the question that National Geographic Emerging Explorer Thomas "T.H." Culhane asked. He saw how people in rain forest villages survived by using every bit of their environment. "It inspired me to rethink urban living along those same ecological principles," Culhane says. In Cairo, he connected with a group called the Zabaleen people who lived in a similar way. They collected the city's garbage by hand. They looked for ways to reuse, recycle, and resell as much waste as possible.

Culhane and a volunteer move a solar water heater into a Cairo neighborhood.

The Zabaleen collected plastic materials. Then they washed the materials and used the sun to dry them for recycling. Culhane began to think about how to use the sun for other things. He knew there was a need for ways to heat water. He developed plans for a simple solar water heater built from recycled materials. (You can see part of his invention in the smaller picture to the left.) It uses plastic water bottles to hold water to be heated. Since 2003, more than 30 water heaters have been installed on rooftops in two different Cairo neighborhoods. Culhane selected the Zabaleen neighborhood and the neighborhood of Darb Al-Ahmar. The two groups work together to share expertise and solve common problems.

CONNECTING PEOPLE AND IDEAS

Connecting people and ideas to solve problems is Culhane's goal. So he started the nonprofit organization Solar CITIES. The organization provides money and basic plans. Then, local people add their skills and creative ideas. People use recycled materials and their own labor to create solar water heaters they can afford.

Solar CITIES also helps people in Kenya recycle food wastes into gas for cooking and heating. Culhane got the idea from working with rural people in India. He developed machines called biogas reactors to turn the food waste into gas. The reactors use **microbes**, tiny organisms such as germs, taken from animal stomachs. "In 24 hours, you've got 2 hours of cooking gas from yesterday's cooking garbage," he noted.

Culhane's energy ideas are now spreading. The Solar CITIES team uses the Internet to explain the system. Biogas reactors have been installed in Kenya, Tanzania, Israel, Botswana, and other countries. The team also posts videos, writes a blog, and connects on social networking sites. In this way, people around the world can add their own ideas. They build on the Solar CITIES project's experience. As Culhane says, "It's just a matter of connecting and letting our collective intelligence work."

Students get a close-up look at a biogas reactor used at their school.

Groups such as Solar CITIES are helping people use the planet's energy resources wisely. Their goal is to improve the lives of people who have little access to more costly energy sources.

Explore the Issue

1. **Identify Problems and Solutions** Why did T. H. Culhane establish the Solar CITIES project?

2. **Make Inferences** How do Culhane's ideas and inventions benefit the people of Cairo and Kenya?

A fellow Emerging Explorer at Kuyha Dream School in Kenya, Culhane demonstrates an in-sink food grinder. The grinder can turn food scraps into fuel and fertilizer.

"In 24 hours, you've got 2 hours of cooking gas from yesterday's cooking garbage."

—T.H. Culhane

Go on an Energy DIET

—and report your findings

You don't have to be an inventor to use energy wisely. You just have to care—and get involved. You can identify many ways to save energy at home and at school. By going on an energy diet and taking steps to use less energy you can make a big difference.

IDENTIFY

- Make a list of all the ways you use energy at home and at school.

- Talk with your family and classmates to brainstorm ideas for ways to save energy.

- Do research on the Internet to learn about steps you can take to use less energy.

- See if your local government or power company has ideas for saving energy.

ORGANIZE

- Form a team with 3 to 5 classmates and review National Geographic's Great Energy Challenge.

- Decide what energy-saving steps you will add to your diet each week.

- Check in every week and decide which actions you actually completed.

High school students work on a project to create a solar car.

DOCUMENT

- Make a list of energy use at the beginning of the diet and changes you will make to use less energy.

- Check the boxes of the actions you have completed on the Great Energy Challenge worksheet.

- Record members of your team discussing their experiences on the energy diet.

SHARE

- Use your photos and recordings to create a multimedia presentation about your energy diet to share with your class.

- Write and perform a skit for your class or a school assembly about ways to save energy.

- Create public service announcements to encourage others to take specific steps to save energy. Share them at your school or a local radio station.

Research & WRITE
Argument

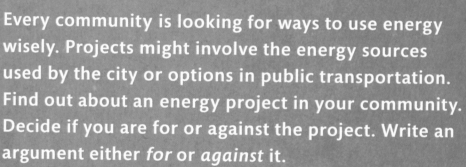

Write an Argument

Every community is looking for ways to use energy wisely. Projects might involve the energy sources used by the city or options in public transportation. Find out about an energy project in your community. Decide if you are for or against the project. Write an argument either *for* or *against* it.

RESEARCH

Use reliable sources such as local media or government sources to research and answer these questions:

- How will the project affect the community's energy use?
- What are the claims, or arguments, in favor of the project?
- What are the counter-claims, or arguments, against the project?

As you do your research, be sure to take notes.

DRAFT

Review your notes and then write a first draft.

- The first paragraph, or introduction, should grab the reader's attention. State your claim, which is your position on the energy sources or public transportation used in your area.
- Briefly explain what the opposing argument is. Then state that you will show why your argument is stronger.
- The second paragraph, or body, should develop your argument. You should present clear reasons and relevant evidence for your claim.
- In the third paragraph, write a conclusion, which should follow from the argument you have presented.

REVISE & EDIT

Read your first draft to make sure that it gives convincing reasons to support your claim.

- Does your introduction clearly state your argument?
- Does the body support your argument with clear reasons and relevant evidence?
- Does your conclusion support your argument about certain energy sources or public transportation in your area?

Revise the argument to make sure you have covered all the points. Then check your paper for errors in spelling and punctuation.

PUBLISH & PRESENT

Now you are ready to publish and present your argument. Print out your paper or write a clean copy by hand. Publish your argument as an opinion piece or a letter to the editor in your school or local newspaper.

reservoir

nonrenewable energy

diversify v., to broaden or add variety to something

fossil fuel n., an energy source, such as coal, oil, or natural gas, formed from the remains of ancient plants and tiny creatures

generator n., a machine that produces electricity

geothermal energy n., heat from inside the earth

hydroelectric power n., electricity created by the energy in moving water; also called *hydropower*

microbe n., a tiny organism, such as a germ

natural gas n., a fossil fuel in the form of a colorless, odorless, and tasteless gas

nonrenewable energy n., an energy source that will be used up, such as coal

renewable energy n., a source of power that can never be used up, such as sun or wind

reserves n., the amount of oil or natural gas that can be recovered from known sources

reservoir n., an artificial lake created behind a dam to store water

revenue n., income used to pay expenses

steppe n., a large grassy plain

turbine n., an engine with spinning blades powered by air, steam, or water pressure

hydroelectric power

renewable energy

fossil fuel

INDEX

SKILLS